Bees of the Invisible

poems by

Maximiliane Donicht

Finishing Line Press
Georgetown, Kentucky

Bees of the Invisible

ACKNOWLEDGMENTS

Previous publications of poems in this chapbook:

"To the Boy Elis" – *Columbia Journal* online (2016)
"Wolpertinger" – *Cold Mountain Review* (2018)
"Salmon" – *Versify* (2018)
"Crewelwork" – *Ecotone* (2018)

Publisher: Leah Maines
Editor: Christen Kincaid
Cover Art: Sir William Jardine
Author Photo: Maximiliane Donicht
Cover Design: Maximiliane Donicht

Printed in the USA on acid-free paper.
Order online: www.finishinglinepress.com
            also available on amazon.com

Author inquiries and mail orders:
Finishing Line Press
P. O. Box 1626
Georgetown, Kentucky 40324
U. S. A.

Table of Contents

This clowder of twitching whiskers is dedicated to the White Moth of Amherst; mother to all our bushy tails; the inimitable Lucie Brock-Broido, whose wicked magick touched so many.

"It is our task to imprint this temporary, perishable earth into ourselves so deeply, so painfully and passionately, that its essence can rise again, 'invisibly', inside us. We are the bees of the invisible. We wildly collect the honey of the visible, to store it in the great golden hive of the invisible."

—Rainer Maria Rilke in a letter to Witold Hulewicz, November 13, 1925 (from Stephen Mitchell's "The Selected Poetry of Rainer Maria Rilke")

Wolpertinger

Come sprinkle salt
on my twitching tail,
dear hunter,

when the barks are kissed
blue, a candle
     in your hair.

        Veiled in susurrus, I balance
        on the bottleneck
   of being

    barely   sit in the blurry skirts
of apricity, in the red braids
of root.

    I have waited
all this time for you
to find me.

       I have waited,
brooding an egg you call
the observable universe

       in a place you call
          the natural world.
    I have felt you

ripen beneath the concave
    of your cinder shell, scrunching

    up against it,
    an eager tiny life.

I have waited
for you to come,
dear hunter.

    Come bury
       your knife.

Apollonian Tea Ceremony
Study of a Chawan

As if the color that doesn't exist
had spilled like amaranth
    over wrought iron, anemone fingers

crawl down
a glazed gray bowl: the invisible
    lips of someone who wore away

the oxblood rim
still thin as absence balancing
    on all edges at once

and within: nimbus
of debris flowers open
    into planets, and from its opal core

the curled sap of reeds
springs up, full without
    needing, its foam like a shrewd surf

I once knelt in,
like the little, bright
    leaves on dunes, who know

more than the animals of children
about the open tumor
    at the center of a great thing's eye,

of the way everything inside
went and will go
    blind and is hummed up

and into the pupil, penumbra
of all lives, and there
    is stirred with a whisk

of one hundred and nine bristles, strung
from bamboo and the little
    left behind.

Quantum Afterglow

There was a first star
that appeared like a needle
in the black felt pocket
of a Copernican greatcoat.

A Flamboyance

After Rainer Maria Rilke's "The Flamingos"

Ornithologists tell us that just under a million alight
        in cold water, wade through swamps on coral stalks
   but well into the billions congregate on front lawns
and flower beds, arching halogen necks,

        not to forget those dangling from trees in living rooms
   or stretching out of crimson drinks on pink
translucent hyperboles;   feast of their barbed tongues
        in ancient Rome, deities, blushing swans pulled

    from rose taffy—they know of our secret reverie, hearts
mown short and crowded with their iron icons
        and wait for us to be gentle between

    waking and thought, beaks hovering above the glassy parchment
of a delta in the early afternoon, palindromical, ready,
        their black brushes dipped in the imaginary

Cera Alba

It was summer then: the bees
all asleep, curled in cornflower laps.

Not for the first time I tried
to guess their names. Their gossip

silenced, I was almost able to hear myself
hum shiny consonants, speak golden

stripes, the intimacy
of fuzzy waists trickling

into my heart like frothed
nectar; the sweet pill found

between poison and flower.
I swallowed it and felt tiny

coned feet settle beside the cluster
where the *I* resides.

Unseen, the hive awakens—abundant

as white clover. A muscle in me
slowly becomes invulnerable

to time. I cut my fingers in the archives
encountering the old movie stub

objects like tiny safety pins or taut
bodies, paper-thin wings. At last

it is winter, which means the workers
are clustering around their queen, shivering

to keep her warm. I, too, flutter ceaselessly
for months, keeping whatever resides

at the center alive, curled up like a pet
by the fire, or mounted posthumously

between my floating ribs.

Furling Tree

Previous carbons sutured by root. New fingers
for birds, premonition soaring through a battery sky.
They used to tell me every book

is written with only four letters, and every letter
is cast from an infinite amount of spyglasses

that only ever show the moment
just before. They have proof, now, that everything is spun
from loosened, gray light. One of these lives

I will tap my most ligneous vein and collect a drum
of warped doorframes, but for now

I am curled tight around another woman's arm,
around her chamber's stale night
in the weft knit of her dying.

Salmon

In some river we tangled   in occult light
     imbibed our barbed love before quick
       the blind fish slipped

back to her silver home. You refused

     to touch me, because it would have been like lying
       (here, a thistly bone settled in).

     That means

our lives brushed like the flick
   of a cat's tail against
     a shin;

it means
the glass blade rings   *hush*
   during the dissection
     of seahorses,

their little chests
   rich as clockwork:
     reporting, repeating.

Final Attempt at Breaking a Neural Pathway

The nuns living in my pockets
shake their bald heads and wrap

themselves tighter in frayed receipts—
They nudge each other and point: watch
how she fumbles past antiquities, digs

as if for answers or her keys
and at the seam touches a thread
of red lint, a grain of sugar, verdigris.

Black Box

Eight minutes
        into the maw
                of noxious agency

the sound of a man's breath is woven
        in the peaks of the French alps.
                It hovers over me

in sleepless dark, beating
        its iron wings.
                They all wonder

why he did it
        but no question fits
                the answer—it was nothing

        personal. The dead hang
                on the other end of a spring, hunting
                        for memories somewhere in a great dusty distance

whistling through breastbones
        mountain ranges, ravines
                and the clenched teeth of a pilot,

magnanimous machine, all function and design
        without command or navigation, wheeling
                and where was his mind, already

                                a dark blue ribbon
                                tucked into the smallest drawer
                                of the earth's spine.

Parakeets

Maybe I shouldn't speak
of anything, but wonder

if the recluse
on Cold Mountain felt it too—

how it is early, too early
to eat, or think, or mourn.

A swarm of monks
flies by, wrapped in their robes

of spring grass. Here
and in another place,

they announce their presence
heatedly, startling across

flushed mist and me,
feathery bells auguring

only that they ring
themselves so shamelessly.

Totenbaum

1
where does the tide settle
between the atom and animal,
between *flutter*
and an intimate definition.

2
around the ankles,
leaving a rim of chalk.

3
my death is mine, you shouldn't
understand it anyway.

4
the tree in the living room, too, is a vessel
for a body, vacant, to crowd
the unfurnished space
in the redefined
object.

5
spiraled paper nautilus,
are you waiting
to liquefy us, for me to slip into
the whorled wound
of your sleep.

6
until we are full
of emptiness, empty
of eyes, that is to say,
until all our mollusks
have left home.

7
how reckless I was to think
time was linear when everything,
even the smallest apparatus,
turns.

8
we take a cypress down
for every one of us.

9
did you know that birds,
like yellow fruit,
are made of thirds.

10
the truth is
I have sensed danger,
and it is nothing
like cold fish.

11
a moth expires inside
a bulb hanging from bare wire
and is reborn a mother.

12
things are living
in corners
of caves
right now.

13
whoever braided the shark-toothed fishwife's hair
into this odd water
we call a fourth dimension:
how many strands did you use
and is all of this really
because you loved her?

Copernican Fata Morgana

From the age of three minutes
to five hundred thousand years
a beardless universe
experienced an era of nowhere
to go on a Tuesday morning.

Turquoise-Browed Motmot

Thank god, the hieroglyphs
have finally returned outside
my window, the sunbird

being very vague once more,
making it hard for me to gather
the subtle rubies of its throat.

They twist their limbs
in the amethyst glimpse
of February, curling themselves

around solar systems of allium
fully efflorescent on the sidewalk despite
my full-fledged porphyrophobia.

I imagine they soaked
in hot springs on some plateau
until their inky contours

ripened from precision—
Did they think about me
at all while they were gone

as I thought of them in the shower;
faint, almost articulating
as long as the water was on.

Crewelwork

My father will join the owls.
His mother came back a crow;
and I, I will be the magpie's

iridescent tail feather,
downcast.

*

Every night, ten thousand wings
knit a black shawl in the sky,
blotting out the cathedral.

They caw on the gable, the seam of their bodies
holding the house together for a moment.

Postcard I Sent Myself from the Future

Inflections of shedding ice, words
and other musical orders
foiled nothing in the end.

But know this:

Rare algae can be found
growing on the cusp
of waking into no language.

Use the brine of them
to cure our self-made carnage,
so future generations will relate
to *ocean, abundant, the left eye*
sees colder colors.

Dark Cloud Constellation

Black wool unwinding from a branch:
the bookish crows rising
from sycamores and flying off
in formation, their movement
a Morse stencil that reads "do not follow us."

Kin

No one here in months

and the beach winterthick with shells

squamous from a neap tide, leviathan's scales,

their strata spring beneath my boots, dozens crunched with

every step. Innumerous smooth homes deserted; a field of pitted

cups, vacant

& abundant like the branches of a bald forest. Each once vesseled

a single hurt-seed, which is to say they are not so different

from us: byzantine sediment biding

to tangle the planet again, wait

for the tide to comb us

seaward.

Numen

Again, this sense that there is still time.
She's dying & a piano

beneath keeps her afloat
as the watchman trumpets

her in, her starchy nightgown stained
cinnamon. The howl again,

night yearning on her, monstrous—

corneous & vague
pinning her down in a desert

she's been before, remembers
hazily as a childhood home,

where her frailty slinks away, wastes
in the mortal sands like milk,

the taste of it teeming
with new mouths.

The Ancient Chinese Philosopher Vanishes

Like pollen to the gold hive,
names ferry through our bodies

until they abscond back into
the milky marrow; names

that no longer quicken
ornamental protoplasm

are merged in absent tissue;
names sail like swans

across seasons,
through the eye

of the ego's needle;
names etch their sounds bluntly

in the pith's rind;
rein hatchling horses into the heart's

jug—those gossamer foals' neighing
a vessel, the fullest kind.

It's Nothing to Worry About

The back of my neck
is a cleft gorge. What thread
could you use to sew me?

That needle will cause light
to come in. Use it.

Jaws of It All

Gathered from Chapter 27 of the I Ching (transl. David Hinton)

To meet it, have no
destination.

Harvest thatch-grass
whole, roots and all

and in this struggle find
only shame. Inhabit

the mulberry, burgeoning
from its seed. Sweep

the dangling jaws
of it all away, sweep

enduring threads
into the hills. Set forth

only after ten years
at the side of a wild-eyed tiger

rabid with slashing hunger
and let him hunt

with his drooping gaze
whatever in you fosters
                you with wild bounty.

Quantum Fluctuation

What luck not to be at
all, not to have eyes
not to see things
paw for milk against
the celestial belly.

Blackbird on Wood

I want to know how and when
they got feathers, or lost them, or altered
their skin's texture

or when we lost ours
and the smoothness of our limbs
warped into limestone;

I'd like to know when I gathered
all this sand in my mouth.

When did our egos, not unlike
them, grow so majestic
and blind, hurling themselves

like exotic darts into glass;
The blackbird that crashed
against our immaculate window

during homeroom, and Ms. McAllister
couldn't stop crying over the angle
of its head, its quiet blue

on wood, or the way its slick wings
jerked on the ground, gleaming.

To the Boy Elis
After Georg Trakl

Blackbird, your forest is falling
into her cool lips
drinker of stone.

Blank spaces, empty
are bleeding
into your flight.

But blue steps softly at night,
whose full rotation depends on purple grapes
and their poor revolution.

Blackbird, your gaze
polishes our daggers, our fins,
how long, Blackbird, have you been?

Your body is a waxen
nun, dipping
her dewy finger in our silence.

Let us enter you softly as an animal
enters a temple or an eye.

Lower yourself, slowly,
as ire drips from the stars, expiring.

Cera Alba

I'd like to inquire
about the bees following me

and how they bottled
their spiral fury
into abdomens whose tremor
can immolate a hornet.

First and last matriarchy,
eusocial order of sisters,
ferocious and surprisingly
tender with sensory bristles
and mouthparts

yet seduced by a legend
of lethal opiate

derived from their favorite
flowering Judas—from within, I am
swarmed by winged jewels,
polished armor, *augochlora*,
until I no longer

feel the strum of my own
existence—how is it that
the deadliest blossom
is also the most delicious?

The answer being motion
equals nonexistence.

Now stretch the void's limb
and touch the farthest reaches
of the mind, oblivious

to the invisible drones who lie
curled up by their tree's roots amid
scraps of pale flower.

Grazing Lunar Occultation

I return to the center of everything
somewhat less magnetic; burnt bulb
now, orbit without sun
and only the bees know where
I have been, what I have undone.

Vis Inertiae
> *To the jaguar at the Museum of Natural History*

You appear
          ears-first,
bulk of muscle with broad shoulders, your jaws

         made for splitting the world's skull, gutted,
         skin stretched & stuffed, as thin morning
         pours over God's chipped incisor,

the distant mountain, spurs
of promise, but the valley still pinched
         in bruises of shade.

Over aeons you have rounded, compacted;
your limbs shorter, face less angular, mossy ponds of your irises
swallowed by sap.

Hardened, here, after all that. Somewhere
you are ready to cannon
into the dilating valley   or hunker down
                    and thaw into the dark
                    drum again

that thrums without glass
or buckets of amber eyes:

         old spark born back
            into the purring pyre, the earth

            alive again, incarnate with the reentry
            of your ore into its vein.

Aftertaste of an Unseen Occurrence

To conceive of tomorrow
is excess, enviable
the pine-toothed forefathers

of feathered things,
who couldn't foresee muscle
falling from their bones

or the clayish audacity
of their rotting hulls. Now
they are salted

away in trees, at lakes
where clouds spill like pinioned
fledglings into troposphere,

their blushing scales
turned storm-
                riddled rind.

The spaces between the birds
headed into Northern
Darkness and the microscopic

parts know who or what leaks
from beyond the event horizon—
hollow-boned phantom lives

rise like phosphene kites, vivid
against the lightlessness inside,
so that we can no longer

ignore the uncanny depth
of the inward eye, which calls my mother's
ultimate disappearance to mind,

the thought tightly slipped
like an unseen grip around the throat
and even asleep

my fingers tangle into nests
until the fear is like fish caught
in tin cans. Last night

over the valley of childhood
a boiling tower knurled
the cracking sky, not quite cloud

but almost swelling
nebula; coral heart of breath
and rain at the center of the universe;

ganglion of antique anatomies
that scaffold our trivially
follicled bodies and span the split

sewn with terrible shields,
our nakedness, and the birds
in between.

Maximiliane Donicht was born and raised in Munich, Germany. She once worked as a pastry chef in Paris, practiced classical Japanese swordsmanship in New York, and now lives in Taipei, where she eats an ungodly amount of purple sweet potatoes. She earned her BFA in Comparative Literature and the Creative Arts with a minor in Psychology at the American University of Paris and holds an MFA in Poetry and Literary Translation from Columbia University. Her poetry has appeared or is forthcoming in *The London Journal of Fiction*, *Bone Bouquet*, *Paris/Atlantic*, and *Cold Mountain Review*. Her translations have been published or are forthcoming in *Gulf Coast Magazine* and online at *The Grief Diaries* and *Columbia Journal*. Her translation of Prof. Dr. Thomas Höllmann's book 'The Chinese Script' was published by Columbia University Press. When she is not writing or translating, she teaches Japanese martial arts. This is her first chapbook.